Burning
the Books
The Guardian Geese
Little Old Boy

For Alison P.

ORCHARD BOOKS
96 Leonard Street, London EC2A 4XD
Orchard Books Australia
14 Mars Road, Lane Cove, NSW 2066
This text was first published in Great Britain in the form of
a gift collection called *The Orchard Book of Roman Myths*,
illustrated by Emma Chichester Clark in 1999.
This edition first published in hardback in Great Britain in 2000
First paperback publication 2001
Text © Geraldine McCaughrean 1999
Illustrations © Tony Ross 2000
The rights of Geraldine McCaughrean to be identified as the author and
Tony Ross as the illustrator of this work have been asserted by them in
accordance with the Copyright, Designs, and Patents Act, 1988.
ISBN 1 84121 887 1 (hardback)
ISBN 1 84121 524 4 (paperback)
1 3 5 7 9 10 8 6 4 2 (hardback)
1 3 5 7 9 10 8 6 4 2 (paperback)
A CIP catalogue record for this book is available
from the British Library.
Printed in Great Britain

BURNING
THE BOOKS
THE GUARDIAN GEESE
LITTLE OLD BOY

GERALDINE McCAUGHREAN
ILLUSTRATED BY TONY ROSS

ORCHARD BOOKS

BURNING THE BOOKS

The Sibyl sat scrawling line after line,
scroll after scroll, writing down her
visions. The future became the present,
then passed into history, but by then she
had written screeds more about days yet
to come. The Sibyl saw the future as a
view from a window, and wrote it down
in her spidery, tangled hand, so that her
prophecies grew like cloth from a loom,
like a scarf from knitting needles.

Nine books of prophecies the Cumaean Sibyl wrote, though that view of hers became less and less pleasant. In the end she rolled up her nine scrolls, laid them in a raffia basket, and carried them all the way to Rome.

She found the place very changed from the days when Romulus had ruled there; a big, prosperous sprawling place now, its map as complicated as a page of handwriting. She found it gloomy, too, its alleyways full of weeping, its children hollow-eyed with worry.

After six good kings had come a seventh: Tarquin the Proud, a despot and a bully. The Roman virtues of Love and Duty were nowhere in his nature, and he ruled Rome as if it were a dog walking at his heel.

Of course the Sibyl knew all this – had seen it coming long before Tarquin had even been born.

"Hail, Tarquin of Rome. I bring books for you to buy," said the bent old woman, shuffling towards the King.

"Books? What do I want with books?" sneered Tarquin. "I know everything worth knowing already."

"What is written in these books no man knows, for they concern the future," said the old woman. "I am the Sibyl of Cumae. I am weary now with writing.

My inkwell is dry. Now I wish to sit and nod in the shade of an olive tree, and think of things past instead of things to come. So pay me one hundred pieces of gold and I will give you these nine books of prophecies, so that you may read what the future holds in store for Rome."

"Who let in this mad old crone?" sniggered Tarquin. "Pay a hundred pieces of gold for some lunatic scribblings? I wouldn't pay one groat to see you eaten by lions. Get out."

From the raffia basket the Sibyl took
one scroll and held it out towards one of
the lamps which lit the room. As it flared
up, she dropped it on the floor of the
throne-room. Every eye watched
it burn, watched the secrets of the
future charring and turning to ash.

"Now there are only eight,
Tarquin. Do you always laugh
at your elders and betters?"

Tarquin curled his lip in contempt (though there was something disturbing about seeing a scroll burn – all those names, those places, those predictions).

"Weather forecasts and gobbledegook," he jeered. "I shall have you put out of doors like a cat."

The Sibyl took a second scroll from her basket and lit it from the embers of the first. It flared up and was gone, ashes scurrying away under the furniture.

No one moved to eject the Sibyl: there was not a man there who had not heard of the ancient Sibyl of Cumae and her writings.

11

"Take care, old witch. You will have nothing left to sell. Already your stock is worth only eighty gold pieces."

"Ah, but the cost has gone up to a thousand," said the Sibyl.

Tarquin grew hot with anger. "What? Pay more for less? What kind of a fool do you think I am? It's eighty or nothing!"

The Sibyl took another scroll and lit it from a guttering candle. The watching crowd gasped and murmured. It was as if the very future itself was going up in flames. Tarquin glimpsed the word 'Rome' as it blackened, smouldered, then burned to ash.

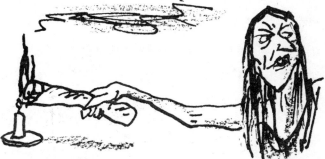

"What kind of fool do you think I am that I will pay a thousand for the ramblings of a mad witch?"

"A fool needs words of wisdom more than a wise man," said the Sibyl. "That is why I came to you. The price is now two thousand."

Tarquin jumped to his feet and lunged about the room. "Do you hear her? Does she insult me as well as bore me with her worthless nonsense?" But the courtiers only stared at the growing heap of ash on the floor – their future, the future of their children, their city, the world, lost to the fire. They were willing Tarquin to pay. When he said, "I won't be held to ransom like this!" they moaned and bit the sides of their hands.

"No!" they groaned as the Sibyl burned another scroll. The room was full of black floating specks now, though Tarquin could not tell them apart from the flecks of anger floating in front of his eyes. She was perfectly right: of course he desperately wanted the scrolls. But then they were his by rights. Everything in Rome was his by rights. "Give me those scrolls!" he raged.

"For three thousand gold pieces I will," said the Sibyl, and burned another scroll.

Tarquin looked around him. He knew they hated him, these toga-clad statesmen and battle-hardened generals. He knew how their fingers itched to draw their daggers against him. He glanced back at the burning vellum and saw his own name written in the Sibyl's scrawl; saw it circled in fire, then burning. He went to stamp out the flames, but the fragile scorched scroll only crumbled to dust under his sandal.

"Very well! Have your extortion
money, you old hag!"

The Sibyl reached for another scroll,
her puckered old face hardened against
his insults.

"All right, I said!" cried Tarquin.
"Stop! Please…the books.
I beg you. Please. Madam.
Lady. Please."

Thus three of the original nine great Sibylline Books were carried for safekeeping to a shrine on Capitol Hill, where the wisest men in Rome studied them, puzzling over the handwriting like men struggling through a thorn hedge.

Tarquin, when his courage and pride returned, sent to have the Sibyl killed, but she was nowhere to be found.

Whenever a problem arose, the people looked to the Sibylline prophecies for an answer. What should they do? What would they do (for the Future was already decided). How would the thing turn out? And whenever they could not find a solution in those three precious scrolls Capitol Hill, they blamed Tarquin. He had robbed them of two-thirds of their future. When they thought about it, he had robbed them of two-thirds of their freedom, too: their money, their civic rights, their reputation as the noblest of city-states. Had the time not come to be rid of Tarquin the Proud?

They scoured the Sibyl's scrolls for an omen, a portent, for encouragement to rise up and rebel. But Tarquin's promised fate had been burned to ashes. Perhaps that was a portent in itself...

So they rose up and rebelled – ousted Tarquin and took back their freedom. As the Sibyl had known all along, men will find in prophecy everything they want to find, whether they have three volumes or nine.

THE GUARDIAN GEESE

Silent as worms, they burrowed under the walls of Veii. Their faces caked black with Etruscan earth, they scraped and scoured and clawed out soil, passing it back down the tunnel in willow baskets.

The city had withstood their catapults and their battering rams, their siege ladders and their fire barrels. So now they were going in underground, to capture the prize Camillus had always dreamed of capturing.

Veii was crammed with Etruscan treasure, and the general who could seize it would surely earn the undying gratitude of Rome!

In the darkest hour, his engineers broke through. They surfaced through the very floor of Juno's temple – and froze, mouths agape. "What is it? An ambush?" Camillus crawled past them impatiently, poking out his head through the stone slabs of the floor.

He was confronted
by a monumental,
ghostly figure. The
goddess Juno towered
over him, fully seven
metres tall, her eyes
seeming to fasten on
him with a queenly
glare. It took him a
moment to realize that
it was only a statue.

"O Juno! Queen of all the Gods! Forgive
me that I enter your temple so rudely,
without priests, without offerings. But
smile on us this night and I swear that I
shall clothe you in silk, house you in a
finer temple by far, and set flocks of geese
to guard you through the lonely night."

The statue's marble face expressed
nothing, of course.

Out of the tunnel behind him,
Camillus's legionaries crept one by one
until they filled every alcove of the temple.
Quietly they unbolted its great doors.
Camillus raised his sword in salute to
the goddess, then led them out on to the

streets to surprise the
Etruscans in their beds.
Veii fell overnight.
Its treasures filled every
cart in the city, and,
all day long,
cargoes of
silver plate
and shields,
parchments and
saddles, amphoras of
wine and bolts of dyed cloth rolled out
of the gates and away down the road
towards Rome: booty for the victorious.

Camillus was revelling in the sight, watching from the city walls, when his men came to him, trembling and tongue-tied. "Don't be angry, sir; it was maybe just the light, sir – a trick of the light, sir, but all of us felt it and we daren't go back in!" They were frightened of their general, but something in the temple of Juno had frightened them even more.

"Just tell me what happened," said Camillus.

"Well, we were washing her – like you ordered, sir! Washing and dressing her. She was covered in cobwebs, and what she was wearing before – well, it was no better than rags – a wicked disgrace, like you said. But then all of a sudden, sir, we couldn't, sir. We just somehow – no saying in words, sir – we just…we just couldn't."

Camillus sighed. Superstitious soldiers could be an infernal nuisance. As he hurried to the temple, he saw the cart-horses outside trembling between the shafts: trembling and snorting and backing away.

A whole detachment of soldiers hovered around the temple door, like men in a trance. But no sooner did he step inside than he understood what had frightened them and the horses. The statue, clean now and dressed in silk, had a quality of holiness about it which made the breath catch in his throat.

Falling on one knee, he bent his head. "O Juno, Bride of Jupiter, Mother of Vulcan, Mistress of Heaven! Is it your wish to go to Rome, and is it I who shall have the honour of escorting you there?"

A soldier dropped his spear. A length of silk slithered to the ground. The great marble figure – every man there saw it – *dipped her head* in a gracious nod and closed her sightless white eyes. "You may," she seemed to say. "I consent. I am ready."

It was such a sight as stuck in each man's mind till the hour of his death. They laid her in the cart as though they were laying down a sleeping child, and when they reached Rome, each man bought, out of his own salary, a goose to loose in the temple of Juno.

High on the slopes of Heaven, Juno smiled to see the welcome Rome gave to her marble likeness. She smiled to see the thankful sacrifices offered up to her by devout, honourable Camillus (who kept all his promises). She smiled to see the geese, her sacred birds, waddle flat-footedly around the temple precincts like busy, officious little priests.

At every honk, citizens turned their heads and looked towards the temple of Juno, remembering to praise the Queen of Immortals. She even smiled to see the doors of Janus's temple closed as the people of Rome put war behind them.

Without a war to fight, however, Rome
thought she could do without her generals.
Camillus, who had been welcomed home
from Veii with garlands and speeches and
gifts, was pensioned off, sent to live in the
country, far away from the city. He went,
but as he went he said, "Beware, Rome.
Beware the Gauls! The Gauls have set
their hearts on Rome."

The Gauls? Why would anyone fear
the Gauls? Those uncivilised louts, oafish
as bears? The Romans looked about them
at their city, their empire, cultured and
sophisticated, prosperous and elegant. How
could a pack of tribal peasants, grubbing a
living on the edge of the world, pose a
threat to Rome?

The Gauls were indeed as savage
as brute beasts: as hungry as well. They
were hungry for the treasures of Rome,
just as Rome had been for the treasures
of Veii. Like wolves drawn by the smell
of cooking, they closed in from all sides
until, one day, the people of Rome
looked out and saw their eyes gleaming
in the dark.

"Camillus! Where is Camillus?" they asked as the Gauls roared in at the gates.

"Send for Camillus! Let him save us!" they cried, choking on the smoke from their homes burning.

"Too late! No one can save us now!" they wailed as they ran for high ground, for Capitol Hill, which rose like a castle keep above the burning city.

The paths up to Capitol Hill were winding and easy to defend. The Gauls, though they washed around the foot of the hill like a flood tide, could not reach the summit where the terrified people cowered in the temples of their gods.

"We can wait!" the barbarians bawled up, in their guttural, ugly language. "Come down and die, or stay up there and starve!" And they prowled the base of the hill, looking for an unprotected path, some secret way up.

A lad found hiding in a grain jar told them what they wanted to know. He thought he could buy his life with the information, but the Gauls killed him anyway, and trod him underfoot as they scrambled up the steeply zigzag path.

The temples of Jupiter and Juno would
be crammed with treasures, crowded with
pretty women, stashed with the prized
possessions carried to the safety of the holy
hill. It would be as easy as cutting the liver
from a chicken...and the liver was always
the sweetest part...

They went up at night, when the
besieged Romans would not be expecting
them. They blacked their faces with
earth and trod softly, so as to keep the
advantage of surprise. Easier to slit the
throats of sleepers than wait till they
woke. The leading man could hear the
snores of sleeping Romans as he reached
the summit, raised an arm, a knee, over
a low stone
parapet. There
was a dagger
clenched between
his teeth.

Then a white
demon reared
up in his face:
a white demon
with an
orange mask.

It swamped him in a hissing roar, then
drove its steel-hard face into his, cracking
the bridge of his nose. The universe seemed
to be full of these monstrous white harpies,
blaring and stabbing, hammering on the
Gauls with wings as hard as sail-booms.
The men first over the wall fell back on to
those behind them, dislodging them from
the steep path and sending them hurtling
down the side of Capitol Hill.

The chorus of shrieking went on and on until every Imperial guard was awake, every dagger drawn. Mothers gathered their children into their arms, men drew their weapons, priests lit beacon fires to see by. The Gauls were driven off, nursing bloody noses and marvelling at what demons the Romans had tamed to guard their holy citadel.

They regrouped, of course, ready to rush the hill at dawn...but dawn found Camillus standing in the ashes of the city gates, a cohort of soldiers close-ranked behind him. The Gauls were trapped like rabbits in the last sheaf of corn.

Once more Camillus was garlanded and fêted and cheered through the streets, though now the noble buildings lay in ruins and the air reeked of smoke. Once again the altar of Juno was heaped with flowers and fruit, while prayers of thanksgiving rose up to Heaven. But the greatest reward went to Juno's sacred geese. Poured out in golden torrents, splashing on to the pavements of the temple, rattling around their paddling, in-turned feet, whole bushels of corn were scattered for the marvellous birds who had saved Rome's holy places from the enemy.

Even the huge, serene statue of the
goddess, Queen of the Gods, seemed to
smile down fondly at the funny, fussy
creatures, while the geese themselves
swung their rear ends with a new swagger,
honking as if to say, "Make way! Make
way! Maaaake way!"

LITTLE OLD BOY

When his plough uncovered the first tuft
of grey, Tarchon thought: A bird. A dead
bird. But when he looked closely, he saw
that the wisps had more the texture of hair
than of feathers.

He dug with his hands, scooping
aside the dry earth. An ear showed itself,
a forehead, an eyebrow. Tarchon hesitated
to dig any further. Had he disturbed the
grave of some murdered man? Then he
touched the scalp and felt it warm under
his hand, and began to dig furiously, with
rising horror and panic.

As soon as the eyes were unearthed, their lids opened. As soon as he uncovered the mouth, it spoke. "Hail, Tarchon. I have little to offer but knowledge, but raise me up and I shall share with you everything I know." It was a boy!

Though his hair was grey and he wore the careworn expression of an old man, Tages was no more than a child! He came to light like some hoard of treasure buried in time of war. Like a treasure chest he was full of precious things. Tarchon took him to the city and introduced him to the officers and senators of Rome: "This is Tages who has come to teach us wonders!"

"Why? Who is he? What family? Who is his father?" asked the senators, affronted by the suggestion that a boy could teach them anything they did not already know.

"My father is a genius," replied Tages in his high, creaking voice, "one of the guardian spirits who keep watch over you from the hour of your birth till the moment of your death. My grandfather is Jupiter himself." Cries of "Blasphemy!" rose to a hundred lips, but there was something so unnerving about those age-milky eyes in that childish face that they let him go on.

"Just as I was buried in the ground, so the future lies hidden in the fabric of Nature. I am come to teach you how to uncover those secrets. Fetch scrolls and let the scribes write down all that I say!"

He told them
how flocks of
birds sometimes
write the future on
the paper sky. He
showed them how
lightning could point
its finger at the truth and
light it up for all to see. He taught them
the magic days of the calendar which, like
pillars in a temple, lend strength to the
year. He told them which dates should be

festival days and
which gods should
be honoured at those
festivals, which rites
best pleased the gods,
which flowers smelt
sweetest in Heaven as
they burned on an altar.

Everything Tages said, the scribes wrote down, and when one scroll was filled, they started on another.

He showed them how chickens grew secrets, like eggs, within their feathery little bodies, and how the truth could be plucked out of the entrails of birds, like fishes out of the sea. In this way a man could discover whether a day would bring success, whether a battle would bring victory, a wedding happiness. In short, Tages taught the Romans all the arts and mysteries of augury and divination.

Twelve books of secrets Tages dictated, and all the while he spoke, he grew older before their very eyes: more sere and colourless and frail. Each day, when he had finished speaking, he would walk out across the ploughed fields around Rome. One day he simply sank down out of sight.

Tarchon ran to the spot, thinking to find the boy had fainted. But the soil had swallowed Tages, as it swallows the rainfall and the dew, down again into the dark ground where all things begin and end.